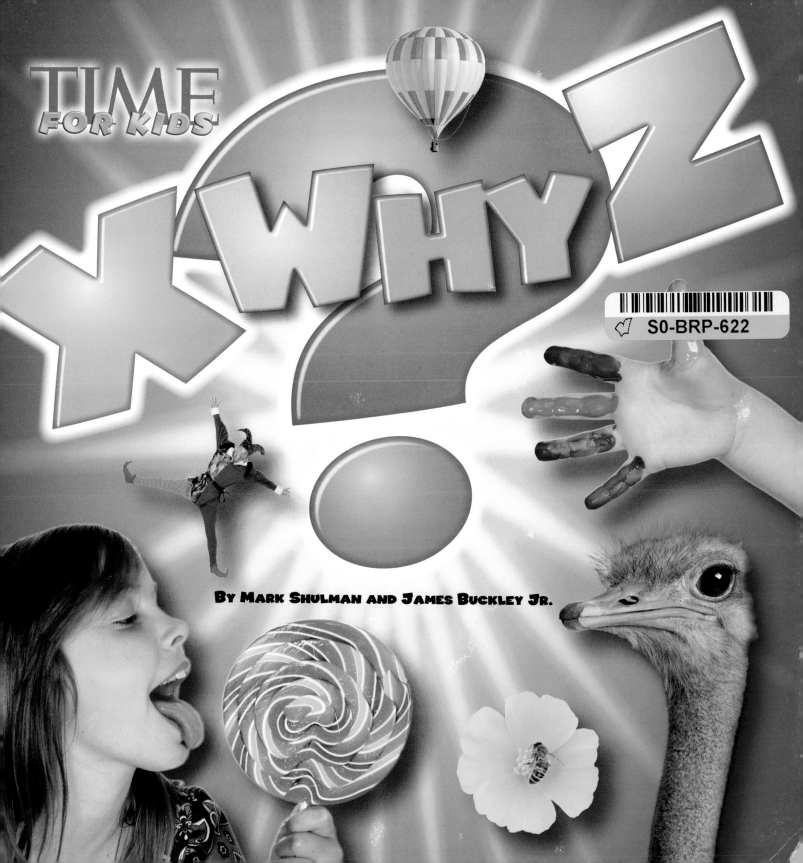

TIME
FOR KIDS

X WHY Z ?

BY MARK SHULMAN AND JAMES BUCKLEY JR.

Time Home Entertainment

Publisher Jim Childs
Vice President, Brand & Digital Strategy Steven Sandonato
Executive Director, Marketing Services Carol Pittard
Executive Director, Retail & Special Sales Tom Mifsud
Executive Publishing Director Joy Butts
Director, Bookazine Development & Marketing Laura Adam
Finance Director Glenn Buonocore
Publishing Director Megan Pearlman
Assistant General Counsel Helen Wan
Assistant Director, Special Sales Ilene Schreider
Senior Book Production Manager Susan Chodakiewicz
Brand Manager Jonathan White
Associate Prepress Manager Alex Voznesenskiy
Associate Production Manager Kimberly Marshall
Assistant Project Manager Stephanie Braga

Editorial Director: Stephen Koepp
Senior Editor: Roe D'Angelo
Copy Chief: Rina Bander
Design Manager: Anne-Michelle Gallero
Editorial Operations: Gina Scauzillo

Created at Oomf, Inc.
www.Oomf.com

By Mark Shulman and James Buckley Jr.
Designed by Bill Madrid
Educational Consultant: Kara Pranikoff
Researcher: Beth Adelman

Special thanks: Katherine Barnet, Brad Beatson, Jeremy Biloon, Dana Campolattaro, Susan Chodakiewicz, Rose Cirrincione, Nataie Ebel, Assu Etsubneh, Mariana Evans, Christine Font, Susan Hettleman, Hillary Hirsch, David Kahn, Amy Mangus, Nina Mistry, Dave Rozzelle, Ricardo Santiago, Adriana Tierno, Vanessa Wu

For information on TIME FOR KIDS magazine for the
classroom or home, go to TIMEFORKIDS.COM
or call 1-800-777-8600.
For subscriptions to SI KIDS, go to
SIKIDS.COM or call 1-800-889-6007.

Published by TIME FOR KIDS Books,
An imprint of Time Home Entertainment Inc.
135 West 50th Street
New York, NY 10020

ISBN 10: 1-61893-372-8
ISBN 13: 978-1-61893-372-0

TIME FOR KIDS is a trademark of Time Inc.

We welcome your comments and suggestions about TIME FOR KIDS Books. Please write to us at:
TIME FOR KIDS Books, Attention: Book Editors, P.O. Box 11016, Des Moines, IA 50336-1016
If you would like to order any of our hardcover Collector's Edition books, please call us at 1-800-327-6388 (Monday through Friday,
7 a.m. to 8 p.m., or Saturday, 7 a.m. to 6 p.m., Central Time).
1 QGT 13

CONTENTS

WELCOME!

WHY DID WE MAKE THIS BOOK?

We wanted to answer your questions!

Asking questions is a great way to learn. This book is filled

with all kinds of questions . . . and answers.

Look for the  boxes to find out even more.

Let's start with the questions from the cover.

Have fun!

WHY DO SKUNKS STINK?

Skunks make a very smelly fluid (*floo*-id) in their body. They spray it to scare away anyone who might hurt them. The stink of skunks can last for many days.

WHY DO RUBBER DUCKS FLOAT?

Something will float when it can push aside the amount of water that weighs as much it weighs. A rubber duck weighs very little. So it only needs to push aside a little water to float.

WHY DOES ICE CREAM MELT?

Cold ice cream takes energy from the warm air around it. The energy warms up the frozen parts of ice cream. The ice inside those parts turns to water … and soon the ice cream is a gooey mess. Eat up!

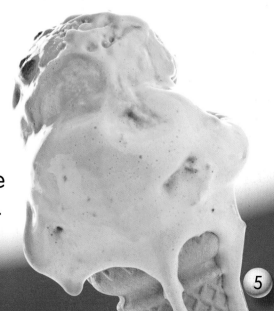

HUMAN BODY

The human body is an amazing machine.

It works hard to keep you safe and healthy.

Give your body a big hand!

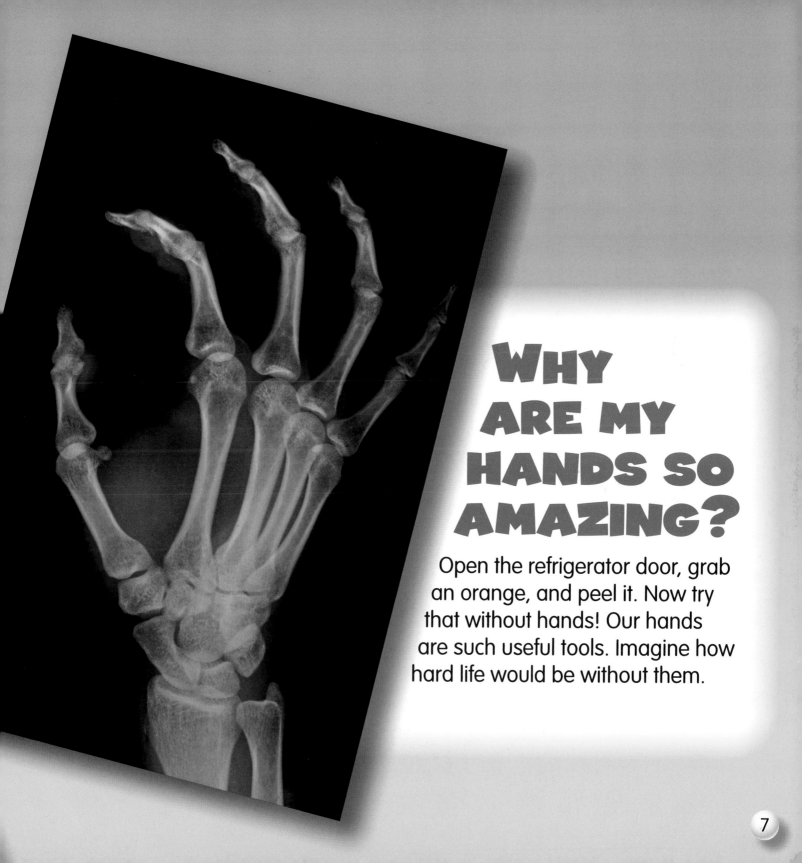

WHY ARE MY HANDS SO AMAZING?

Open the refrigerator door, grab an orange, and peel it. Now try that without hands! Our hands are such useful tools. Imagine how hard life would be without them.

WHY DOES MY LEG FALL ASLEEP?

Your body has many nerves. Nerves are like wires that send messages to your brain. If you sit the wrong way, a nerve gets pinched and the message can't get through. Then you can't feel your leg. When you move again, your leg tingles!

WHY? FACT:

Hamsters don't blink. They wink, one eye at a time.

8

WHY DO I HICCUP?

There is a muscle near your lungs that helps you breathe. When that muscle vibrates, it pushes air out with a pop. Hiccup!

WHY DO I BLINK MY EYES?

When you blink your eyes, you clean them. Blinking also keeps your eyes wet. Eyes don't feel good when they are dry. Most people blink every four seconds!

WHY DO I HAVE FINGERNAILS?

Nails protect the tips of your fingers and toes. Fingernails make it easy to scratch an itch, peel a fruit, untie a knot, and so much more.

XWHYZ FACT:

In Britain, goosebumps are called "chicken skin."

WHY DO I GET GOOSEBUMPS?

Goosebumps help your skin keep warm. Your hair stands up to protect your skin from cold air. Each tiny hair makes one bump.

WHY DO I HAVE EYEBROWS?

Eyebrows protect your eyes from sweat and rain. They help stop water from rolling into your eyes. Eyebrows help keep the sun out, too.

WHY DO I FEEL SICK TO MY STOMACH?

Your body wants to get rid of germs, bad food, and other nasty stuff. That's why when you're not feeling well, you may vomit. A fast or bumpy ride can also shake up food, and make you throw up.

WHY DO I HAVE BOOGERS?

Boogers are dried mucus (*myoo*-kus). Mucus is sticky stuff in your nose that catches dirt, dust, and germs before you can breathe them into your lungs. If you think boogers are bad, think about what they keep out of your lungs!

WHY DO CUTS BLEED?

Blood travels in thin tubes called vessels. When skin gets cut, blood vessels usually break open and blood comes out. If you cover the cut, the vessel will close again.

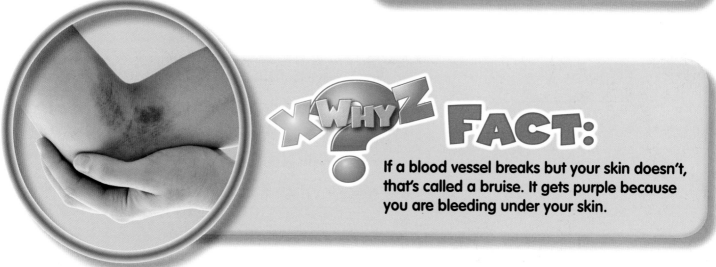

XWHYZ FACT:

If a blood vessel breaks but your skin doesn't, that's called a bruise. It gets purple because you are bleeding under your skin.

WHY DOES HAIR TURN WHITE?

The real color of hair is white! When you are young, your hair has pigment in it. This pigment gives your hair its color. When you get older, the pigment stops working. That's when hair starts to turn white.

WHY DO MY TEETH FALL OUT?

Kids lose baby teeth to make room for adult teeth. All 20 of your baby teeth will fall out. New, larger teeth will grow in. If you take care of them, you may be able to keep those adult teeth forever!

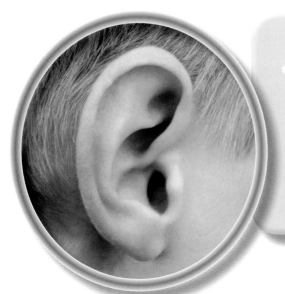

FACT:

Ear wax works like tears. Without wax, our ears would be dry and itchy. It's not gross—it's good!

WHY DO I HAVE A BELLY BUTTON?

Before you were born, you got your food and oxygen through an umbilical (um-*bill*-uh-kul) cord. The cord attached you to your mother. Your belly button is where the cord used to be.

15

WHY DO I YAWN?

Experts say that when you are tired, you breathe more slowly. When that happens, your body does not get enough air. The yawn is a big gulp of air.

WHY DOES MY HEART POUND WHEN I'M SCARED?

When you are scared, your heart pumps blood harder. This gives you the energy you need to run away from danger. When you calm down, so does your heart.

WHY DO I CRY WHEN I'M SAD?

Your brain knows when you feel sad. It sends a message to your body to produce tears. Some scientists think that crying may be our body's way of helping us to feel better.

 FACT:

Everybody gets angry now and then. It can be a normal way to feel. Talking to an adult about your anger may make you feel better.

WHY DOES MY STOMACH RUMBLE?

Your stomach makes juices to help digest food. Those juices help turn food into vitamins and energy. When your stomach is empty, the juices work—even if there's nothing to digest. The rumble means, "Hey, your stomach is empty!"

WHY DO I HAVE TO EAT VEGETABLES?

Vegetables are some of the best foods for you to eat. They have important vitamins, minerals, and fiber that are not in other foods. Vegetables make your body healthy and strong. They will make you feel great, too!

WHY DOES SOME FOOD TASTE GOOD?

Your tongue is covered with tiny bumps called taste buds. Taste buds tell your brain which foods taste good. When something tastes bad, the taste buds tell your brain that, too!

ANIMALS

Animals come in all shapes, sizes, and colors.

You'll meet many interesting animals in this part of the book.

It's totally wild!

WHY DO PARROTS TALK?

Parrots copy the sounds they hear.
They can repeat words that you say.
Sometimes they even use the words
in just the right way!

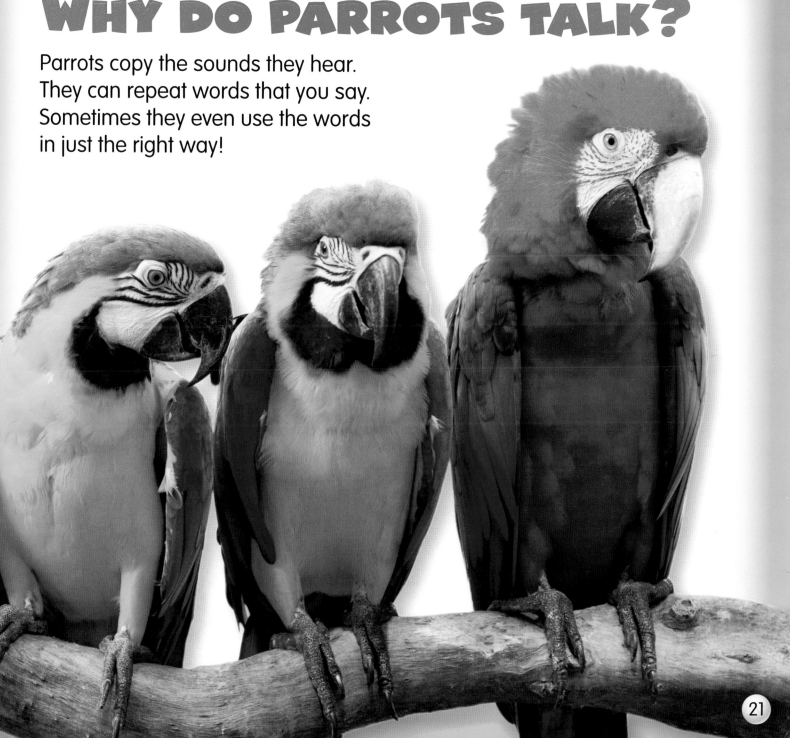

WHY DO CATS PURR?

Purring makes cats feel good.
Cats will purr when they are happy.
Kittens purr to tell their mom, "I'm okay!"

X WHY Z FACT:

Raccoons and guinea pigs purr, too.

WHY DON'T CATS LIKE WATER?

Most cats cannot swim.
They do not like the way
water feels on their fur.
Cats prefer to lick their fur clean.

WHY DO CATS LICK YOU?

Cats lick people to show
they care. It's like a mother
cat cleaning her kitten.

WHY DO DOGS DIG HOLES?

Long ago, dogs did not live with humans. They lived in the wild. Those wild dogs dug holes for shelter, and to hide food. Your dog is acting like those dogs from long ago.

WHY DO DOGS BARK?

Dogs bark to get attention. They may be saying, "Hello!" or "Watch out!" or "Look over here!" Some dogs bark just because they are happy.

WHY DO SOME DOGS CHEW ON THINGS?

Dogs chew on things for a few reasons. They may want to learn about the thing in their mouths. Dogs also chew if they are bored, or to make their teeth feel good.

XWHYZ FACT:

In Alaska, strong dogs pull sleds across ice and snow.

ANIMALS

WHY ARE FLAMINGOS PINK?

Flamingos are not born pink. Baby flamingos are gray and white. The shrimp they eat turns their feathers pink over time.

XWHYZ FACT:

The ostrich is the world's biggest bird. It can be taller than a basketball player!

WHY CAN HUMMINGBIRDS STOP IN THE AIR?

Hummingbirds can beat their wings more than 50 times every second. This makes them powerful flyers. They can slow down and stop in the air. They can even fly backward.

WHY CAN BATS FLY SO WELL IN THE DARK?

Bats use their ears to find their way in the dark. They make noises as they fly. The noises bounce off hard objects like walls. Bats know to fly away from those hard objects.

ANIMALS

WHY DO MALE LIONS ROAR?

Male lions roar to say, "This place is mine!"
Other lions hear the roar and know to stay away.
A lion fiercely guards its home area.

WHY DO TIGERS HAVE STRIPES?

Tigers hunt in the tall grass.
Their stripes make it harder for other
animals to see them well. When
other animals finally see the tiger . . .
they need to run fast!

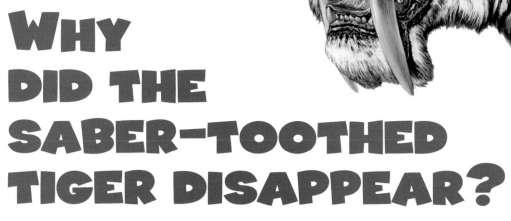

WHY DID THE SABER-TOOTHED TIGER DISAPPEAR?

The last saber-toothed tigers died 12,000 years ago. Experts believe humans and tigers were hunting the same animals. They had to compete with each other for food. Or maybe the tigers were hunted by humans.

X WHY Z FACT:

No two leopards have exactly the same pattern of spots. That's how you can tell leopards apart.

WHY DO SHARKS ATTACK?

Sharks are predators. They hunt other animals for food. They eat sea mammals and fish. Sharks don't eat humans. People do not taste good to them.

XWHYZ FACT:

Check out these walrus tusks! They can be three feet long. Walruses use their tusks for digging holes in ice or to fight.

WHY DO DOLPHINS JUMP OUT OF THE WATER?

Jumping lets dolphins breathe air. It carries them far using less energy than swimming. Jumping is also a way dolphins signal one another.

WHY DO WHALES BLOW WATER FROM THEIR HEADS?

Whales (and dolphins) are mammals. Like all mammals, whales need to breathe air. They swim to the water's surface. When they breathe out, water and air shoots from their blowholes.

WHY DO SPIDERS SPIN WEBS?

Spiders make webs to catch food. Insects get trapped in the sticky webs. Then spiders wrap up the insects to eat later.

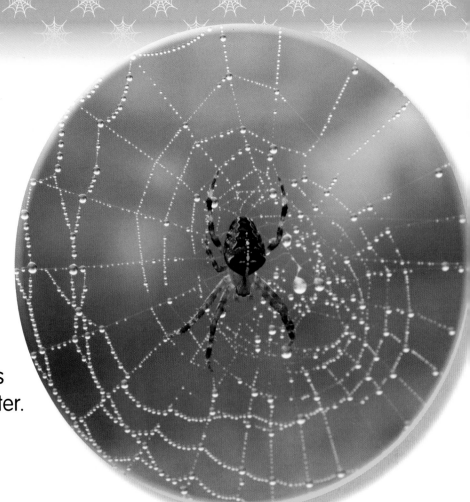

WHY DO CRICKETS CHIRP?

Crickets chirp to help them find mates. Males chirp loudly to show off for females.

WHY DO BEES MAKE HONEY?

Bees make honey for winter eating. They collect nectar from flowers in the spring and summer. They store the sweet liquid in their hive, where it becomes honey.

X-WHY-Z FACT:

Spiders are not insects. They are arachnids (uh-*rack*-nids). Spiders have eight legs, and insects have six. Most spiders are harmless.

8 legs

6 legs

NATURE

Nature is a living thing.

It is always changing and growing.

Watch the world around you closely.

Nature will always surprise you!

WHY DO BUTTERFLIES LIKE FLOWERS?

Butterflies drink nectar (*nek*-tur) from flowers. Nectar is a liquid (*lik*-wid) that is full of sugar, so it is very sweet.

WHY DO GRAPES TURN INTO RAISINS?

Grapes become raisins when they dry in the sun. Grapes have a lot of water and sugar in them. The hot sun removes water from the grapes.

WHY DOES FRUIT TASTE SO GOOD?

Fruit tastes good so that animals will eat it. When the animal is done eating, the pits or other seeds are dropped on the ground in a new place. More fruit grows in the new location.

WHY DO PEACHES HAVE PITS?

All fruits have seeds. The large, hard peach pit is a seed from the peach tree. If you plant a peach pit, you can grow a peach tree.

WHY DO PUMPKINS HAVE STEMS?

Pumpkins grow on vines. The stem is where the pumpkin connects to the vine. When the pumpkin is picked, the stem remains. The stem that's left on the pumpkin can be used as a handle!

WHY ARE PEPPERS DIFFERENT COLORS?

These large peppers are called bell peppers. Bell peppers are green when they are not ripe. If the peppers stay on their vines until they are ripe, they will change colors. Most ripe bell peppers are red, orange, or yellow.

WHY IS A TOMATO A FRUIT?

Two rules will help you identify fruit. 1) Fruits come from plants that grow flowers. 2) Fruits have seeds. Tomatoes have seeds, and the tomato plant grows flowers. Green beans and corn kernels are really fruits, too!

WHY ARE VEGETABLES KEPT IN THE REFRIGERATOR?

Vegetables continue to ripen even after they are picked. The cold air in a refrigerator slows down ripening. If you don't keep vegetables cold, they will turn rotten faster. Yuck!

X WHY Z ?

FACT:

Some of the world's biggest and strongest animals eat only plants. The elephant, hippo, buffalo, and rhinoceros eat only vegetables every day.

WHY DO TREE LEAVES CHANGE COLOR?

During the spring and summer, leaves are filled with green chlorophyll (*klor*-oh-fill). The chlorophyll helps the trees make food, and it makes the leaves look green. In the colder fall weather, leaves lose their chlorophyll and show their bright colors.

XWHYZ FACT:

Walnuts are the seeds of the walnut tree. Almonds are the seeds of the almond tree. Acorns are the seeds of the oak tree.

WHY DO SOME TREES STAY GREEN ALL WINTER?

Trees that do not change color are called evergreens. Their thick, needle-shaped leaves can stand up to cold winters. They won't dry out and die. Pine trees are a common type of evergreen.

WHY DO TREES HAVE RINGS?

Water helps trees grow. Xylem (zy-lem). is the part of the tree that carries water from the roots to the leaves. When you cut a tree down, you can see where a new ring of xylem grew each year. You can learn the tree's age by counting the rings.

WHY DO ROSES HAVE THORNS?

Sharp, pointy thorns help a rose protect itself. Animals are attracted to the rose's bright color and sweet smell. Thorns poke the animals that try to eat the rose.

WHY CAN MUSHROOMS LIVE IN DARK PLACES?

Plants need sunlight to make their own food. Mushrooms don't make their own food. They get their food from dead plant and animal matter in the soil. That's why they don't need light.

WHY DO MOST FLOWERS SMELL SO GOOD?

The smell invites bees and other insects to visit the flowers. Flowers make pollen, a powder that sticks to the insects' bodies. As the insects travel from flower to flower, they spread the pollen. This helps flowers grow.

XWHYZ FACT:

Trees and other green plants release oxygen into the air. Oxygen is what humans and other animals breathe. We couldn't live without it. Thank you, plants!

NATURE

WHY DO DANDELIONS TURN FUZZY?

A new dandelion has a yellow flower. When the dandelion gets old, the flower turns fuzzy and white. At the bottom of each fuzzy bit is one seed. When the wind blows, the fuzz flies into the air, carrying the seed. If the seed lands in good dirt, a new dandelion seed can grow.

44

WHY IS GRASS GREEN?

Plants that are green contain chlorophyll. Chlorophyll is a green chemical that helps plants turn sunlight into food.

WHY DO WE PULL OUT WEEDS?

A weed is a plant you don't want in your garden or lawn. Weeds get in the way of the plants you want to have. Weeds take water and block sunlight. They are not nice to look at. Out they go!

EARTH & SPACE

You live on a planet called Earth.

The Earth travels around the sun.

The sun travels around the universe.

What an amazing ride!

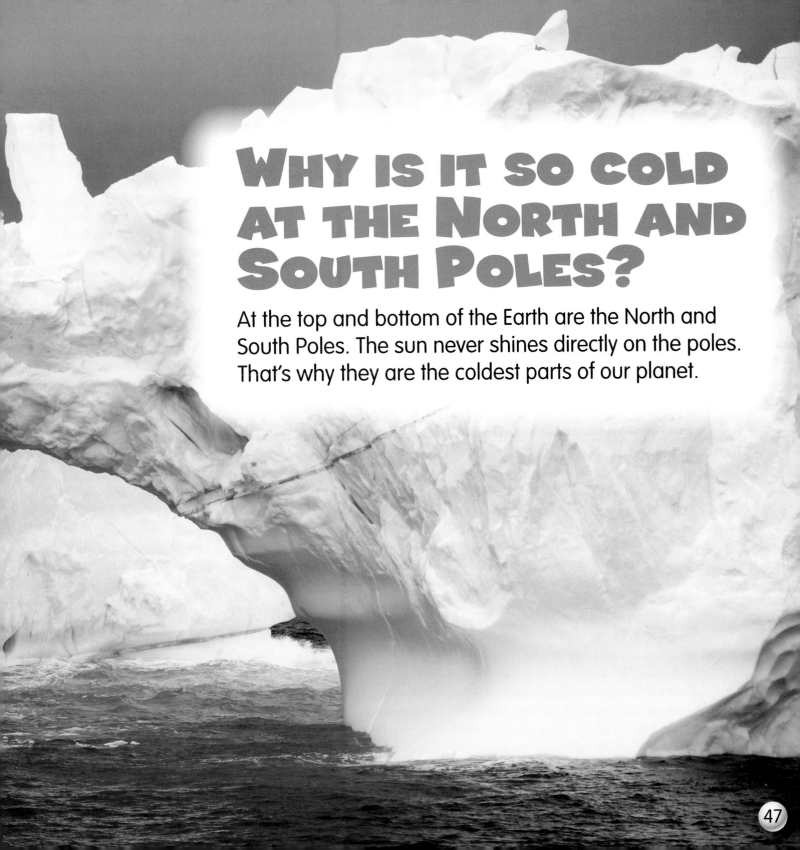

WHY IS IT SO COLD AT THE NORTH AND SOUTH POLES?

At the top and bottom of the Earth are the North and South Poles. The sun never shines directly on the poles. That's why they are the coldest parts of our planet.

WHY DOES IT RAIN?

When water is warmed by the sun, it turns into an invisible gas called vapor (*vay*-per). Vapor rises with warm air. In the sky, vapor cools and turns into tiny water droplets. This is how clouds are formed. When the droplets get too heavy, they fall to the ground as rain.

WHY DOES SNOW FALL?

Snow is created the same way as rain. Cold air makes the water vapor in clouds heavy. The water vapor turns to water drops. If it is a very cold day, the drops will freeze in the air and turn into snowflakes.

XWHYZ FACT:

Hail forms when rain freezes. Hailstones can be as big as golf balls!

WHY DOES THE WIND BLOW?

Warm air rises and cold air sinks. When air gets warm from the sun, it becomes lighter and rises. Cooler air rushes in to replace it. The movement of all this air is called wind.

WHY DO RIVERS FLOW?

Rivers begin in mountains. Rain and melted snow flow downhill, forming rivers and creeks. Where the land is flat, water forms puddles, ponds, and lakes.

WHY DO OCEANS HAVE WAVES?

Most waves are caused by the wind blowing on the water's surface. Also, the gravity of the moon and sun can act like magnets that push and pull the water. When this happens, it's called a tide.

WHY IS THE EARTH ROUND?

Crush a piece of paper in your fist. Now the paper is a ball. Why? Because you pushed on all sides at the same time.

A planet's gravity works like your fist. It pulls every part of the planet to the center with the same power. What is left is a ball, or sphere [*sfeer*].

WHY DO SOME MOUNTAINS HAVE POINTED TOPS?

A pointed top tells us that the mountain is young. Older mountains have rounded tops. Rain, snow, and wind smooth out pointy mountain tops over time.

WHY DO VOLCANOES ERUPT?

Volcanoes occur where there are holes in the Earth's crust. The Earth's crust is made up of huge slabs of rock, called plates. Under the plates is magma, which is hot, melted rock. The plates are always moving, and sometimes magma escapes.

WHY IS IT SO HOT IN THE DESERT?

Deserts are hot because they get little rain. Water would help cool the sun's heat. Sometimes tall mountains on the edge of a desert will block clouds from bringing rain. Those deserts are always dry.

WHYZ FACT:

The hottest desert in America is in Death Valley, in southern California. It can be as hot as 120 degrees there in summer!

WHY ARE MANY BEACHES MADE OF SAND?

Water and wind slowly erode, or wear away, rocks. Over time, the rocks get smaller and smaller until they become tiny grains of sand.

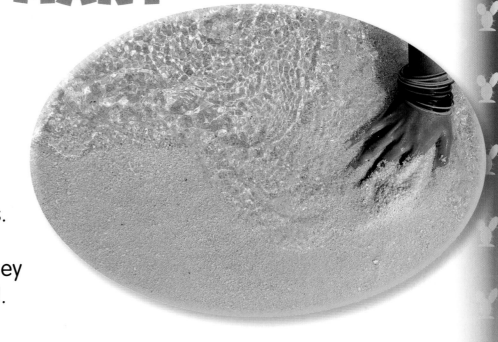

WHY CAN A CACTUS LIVE IN THE DESERT?

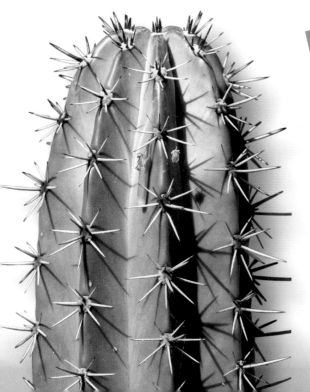

A cactus doesn't need much water to live. It stores what little water it gets in its thick body. A cactus has sharp spines to keep thirsty animals from stealing its water.

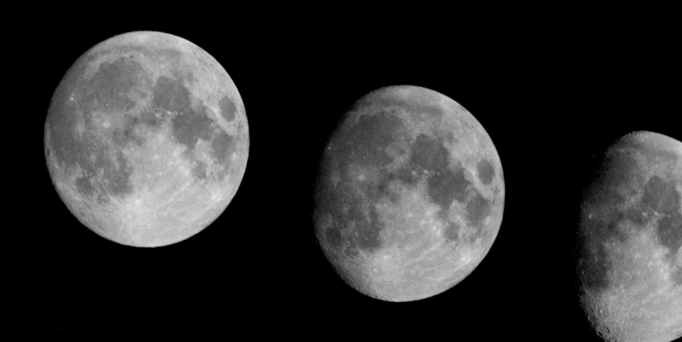

WHY DOES THE MOON SEEM TO CHANGE SHAPE?

One side of the moon always faces the sun, and one side is always dark. Here on Earth, we can only see the part of the moon that is lit by the sun. For a few days every month, we see the whole lit side, and we call it a full moon. The rest of the month, we only see part of the lit side, so the moon looks smaller. When we can't see any of the lit part, we call that a new moon.

WHY DOES THE MOON SHINE AT NIGHT?

The moon has no light of its own. The moon is bright because the sun is shining on it. In the daytime, it is hard to see the moon. But at night, when the sky is dark, the moon's bright glow appears.

XWHYZ FACT:

Humans landed on the moon for the first time in 1969. Footprints they made are still there! Why? Because there is no wind in space to blow them away!

WHY IS THE SUN SO HOT AND BRIGHT?

Our sun is a star. Stars are huge balls of fiery gas and plasma [*plaz*-muh]. We can feel the sun's heat and light even though we are 93 million miles away. That's because the sun is really enormous. One million Earths could fit inside the sun.

WHY DOES THE SUN MOVE IN THE SKY?

Each day, the sun seems to move across the sky. It's really the Earth that's moving. The Earth is spinning like a top. It takes one day for the Earth to spin once around. When your part of the Earth is facing the sun, it's called daytime. When your part of the Earth is facing away from the sun, it's called night.

X WHY Z FACT:

Shooting stars are not stars! They are actually meteors— huge balls of rock and ice burning up in the sky as they fall to Earth.

WHY ARE SOME STARS BRIGHTER THAN OTHERS?

Stars of all sizes fill the sky. The larger stars look brighter. So do the stars that are closest to Earth. Starlight can travel far. A star that looks small and dim may really be a giant star that is billions of miles away.

INVENTIONS

Humans have always invented tools to make life easier.

Inventions can make our lives more fun, too.

Think about all your favorite inventions!

WHY CAN HOT AIR BALLOONS FLY?

Hot air rises. A heater fills the balloon with hot air, causing the balloon to rise.
Wind carries the balloon through the air.

WHY DO FIREFIGHTERS USE FIRE HYDRANTS?

Fire hydrants are like water faucets. Firefighters connect hoses from their fire engines to the hydrants. Then the water comes out of the hoses to fight the fire.

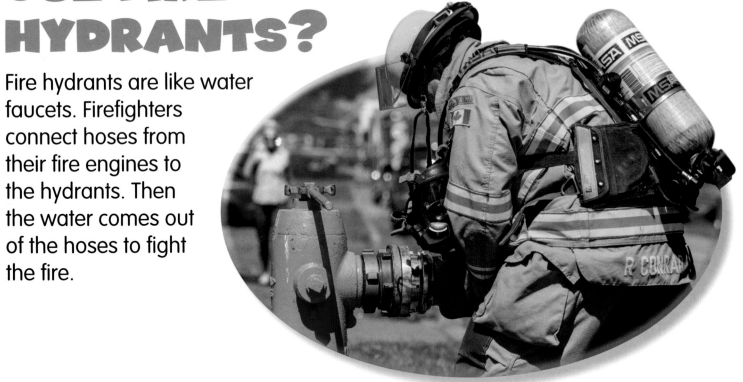

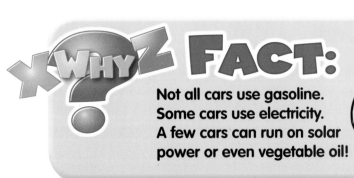 **FACT:**

Not all cars use gasoline. Some cars use electricity. A few cars can run on solar power or even vegetable oil!

WHY ARE SCHOOL BUSES YELLOW?

Yellow is an easy color to see, even in bad weather. The bright color warns drivers to look out for children.

WHY ARE SOME MOTORCYCLES SO LOUD?

Many riders like their motorcycles to be loud. A loud engine can help keep a rider safe. A motorcycle can be hard for car drivers to see. The roar says, "A motorcycle is coming."

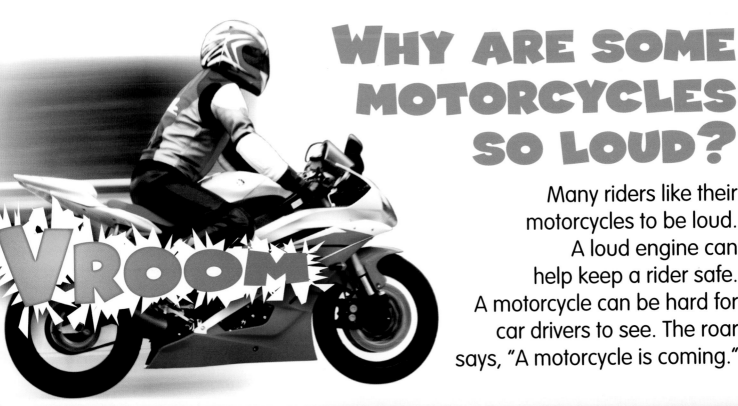

VROOM

WHY DO AIRPLANES STAY UP IN THE AIR?

Kites, birds, and airplanes ride on the air the way surfers ride on water. Engine power pushes the plane forward. Air rushing over and under the wings pulls the plane up and keeps it afloat.

XWHYZ ? FACT:

The Wright brothers made history back in 1903 when they invented the first airplane. The airplane flew for only 12 seconds.

WHY CAN HELICOPTERS FLY?

A helicopter's rotors (*ro*-turs) do two things. First, they spin so fast that they push the helicopter up, the same way a fan has the power to push air. Once the helicopter goes forward, the rotors act like the wings of an airplane, riding the air that flows over and under the blades.

WHY CAN HANG GLIDERS FLY WITHOUT AN ENGINE?

Gliders float on cushions of hot air that rise up from the ground. To steer the gliders, pilots move their bodies.

INVENTIONS

WHY IS A CANOE DIFFERENT FROM A KAYAK?

A canoe is an open boat.
A kayak is a covered boat.
A kayak will not fill with water,
even if it turns over.

WHY DON'T SUBMARINES SINK TO THE SEA BOTTOM?

Submarines are boats that go underwater. The air inside them helps them to float. To lower the submarine, tanks are filled with water. The more water in the tanks, the more the sub sinks. Water is let out to make the sub rise.

WHY CAN SAILBOATS MOVE WITHOUT A MOTOR?

Wind fills the boat's sails and pushes it through the water. The sailboat captain moves the sails to "catch" the wind. Many people have gone around the world using sails and no motor.

FACT:

A racing boat zipping across the water is as fast as a race car.

G·351

WHY WERE THE FIRST COMPUTERS SO BIG?

The first computers were as long and heavy
as two school buses. The inside parts were very large.
No one knew how to make them smaller.
It took many years to learn how to make small computer parts.

X WHY Z?

FACT:

The first e-mail message was "QWERTYUIOP." Why? Look at a computer keyboard to figure out where that message came from!

WHY DO PHONES GET PLUGGED IN AT NIGHT?

A phone needs electricity to work. That electricity is saved in its battery. As you use your phone, the saved electricity gets used up. To get more electricity, the phone has to be plugged into an electric outlet.

WHY IS THIS CALLED A REMOTE CONTROL?

A remote control is a small machine that helps you control a bigger machine. Control means "take charge" and remote means "from a distance." When you turn on a TV from across the room, you control it from a distance.

WHY DO MICROWAVE OVENS WORK SO QUICKLY?

Microwave ovens don't use regular heat. They use waves of energy that heat water. Most food has water in it. The microwave cooks the water inside food. Regular ovens are slower. Those ovens cook the outside of food first.

WHY CAN HOT AND COLD WATER COME FROM THE SAME FAUCET?

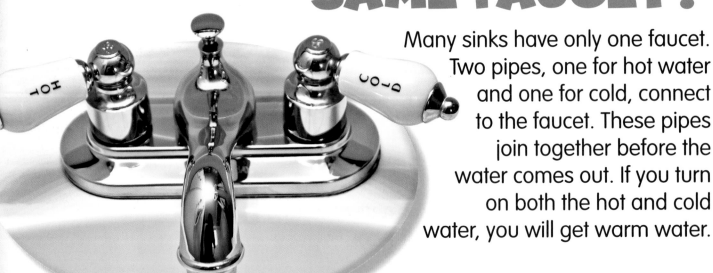

Many sinks have only one faucet. Two pipes, one for hot water and one for cold, connect to the faucet. These pipes join together before the water comes out. If you turn on both the hot and cold water, you will get warm water.

WHY DOES A STOVE GET HOT?

Different stoves heat in different ways. A gas stove makes a fire with natural gas. An electric stove has a metal coil that gets hot. The dials on the stove allow adults to turn the heat up or down. Hands off!

X WHY Z?

FACT:

The ice maker in freezers is not magic. There is a water pipe that goes into those freezers. The cold air turns the water into ice.

PLACES

The world is filled with amazing places.

In this section of the book, you will visit some of them.

Have a great trip!

WHY IS THE GRAND CANYON SO LARGE?

The Grand Canyon, in Arizona, is very wide and deep.
At the bottom of the canyon is the Colorado River. For millions of years, the river has washed away rocks and dirt.
The canyon is the hole dug by the river.

PLACES

WHY WAS THE GREAT WALL OF CHINA BUILT?

The Chinese began building the Great Wall more than 2,000 years ago to keep enemies out of the country. Unfortunately, it did not always work. Still, the wall is a great accomplishment. At 5,500 miles, it is the longest man-made structure in the world.

WHY DID THE ANCIENT GREEKS BUILD THE PARTHENON?

The mighty Parthenon is in Greece. The Parthenon was once a temple. It was built to honor the Greek goddess Athena. The Parthenon is about 2,500 years old. It sits at the top of a hill, looking over the ancient city of Athens.

WHY IS THIS TOWER CALLED THE EIFFEL TOWER?

The Eiffel Tower was designed by Gustave Eiffel. It was finished in 1889. This famous iron tower in Paris, France, is more than 1,000 feet tall. It was the tallest structure in the world for more than 40 years.

X WHY Z FACT:

Big Ben is not the name of this huge tower in London. It's the name of the huge bell inside the tower!

WHY ISN'T THE GOLDEN GATE BRIDGE GOLD?

XWHYZ ? FACT:

The Gateway Arch is in St. Louis, Missouri. It is the tallest man-made monument in the USA.

San Francisco Bay is in California. The place where the bay meets the Pacific Ocean is called the Golden Gate Strait. The famous bridge stretching across the bay is called the Golden Gate Bridge. The bridge is painted orange to help ship captains and airplane pilots see it in the fog.

WHY IS THE EMPIRE STATE BUILDING SO FAMOUS?

The Empire State Building is in New York City. From 1931 to 1972, it was the world's tallest building. It has 102 floors. In the famous movie *King Kong*, a giant gorilla climbs to the top of the building and fights airplanes!

WHY WAS THE WASHINGTON MONUMENT BUILT?

The Washington Monument is in Washington, D.C. The monument was built to honor the first U.S. President, George Washington. It is 555 feet high, which makes it the tallest building in Washington, D.C.

PLACES

WHY ARE SKYSCRAPERS SO TALL?

Strong materials like steel and concrete allow us to build taller and taller buildings. These skyscrapers can fit a lot of people into a small piece of land. Plus, they make cities look impressive.

Some people live on houseboats. These homes float on rivers and lakes. Most houseboats do not travel.

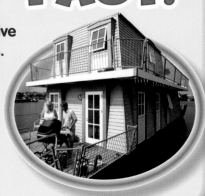

WHY DO IGLOOS KEEP PEOPLE WARM?

A house made of ice does not sound warm. But people who live in frozen places can make an igloo very comfortable. A fire can warm the small space, but it will not melt the ice walls. The igloo also blocks the freezing wind.

WHY DO SO MANY HOUSES HAVE A POINTED ROOF?

A pointed roof is shaped like the letter A. This kind of roof protects the house. When it rains, the water runs off and does not make puddles. Puddles on a flat roof could make the roof leak. A pointed roof will protect against snow, too.

WHY IS A GLOBE THE BEST KIND OF WORLD MAP?

The Earth is round, but most maps are flat. Those flat maps can't exactly match the size and shape of countries and continents. The best way to see how the world is put together is by looking at a round globe.

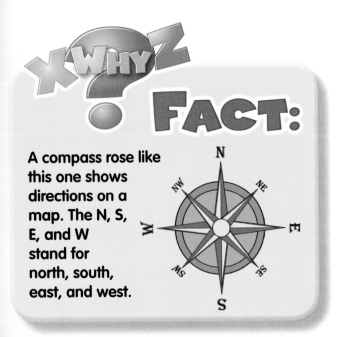

XWHYZ ? FACT:

A compass rose like this one shows directions on a map. The N, S, E, and W stand for north, south, east, and west.

WHY CAN A GPS FIND YOU?

A GPS device sends signals to satellites in space. The satellites tell your GPS device where you are on Earth. Then you see your location on a map.

WHY DID PIRATES PUT AN X ON THEIR TREASURE MAPS?

The idea of an X marking the site of buried treasure came from fictional stories. There are no examples in history of pirates making such maps. Not many pirates buried treasure, either.

HISTORY

Inside the word "history" you can find "story."

Our history is everything we know about our past.

It's the best story ever!

George Washington

WHY WAS MOUNT RUSHMORE BUILT?

Mount Rushmore was carved to honor four U.S. presidents. Each of the heads is as tall as a six-story building. Washington's nose is as long as a minivan!

Thomas Jefferson

Teddy Roosevelt

Abraham Lincoln

WHY DID PEOPLE LIVE IN CAVES?

Early people rarely used caves as permanent homes. Some people moved from place to place following animals they depended on for food. They used caves as temporary shelter.

WHY DID PEOPLE START TO TRADE THINGS?

Long ago, there were no stores. If you wanted something, you had to grow it or make it. So people traded what they had for the things they needed. For instance, a hunter might trade meat for a farmer's grain.

WHY DID EARLY PEOPLE FORM TRIBES?

Early people formed groups, or tribes, to make their lives easier and safer. People living in tribes shared food and skills. They also protected one another. It is easier to stay alive when everyone helps out.

WHY DID EGYPTIANS MAKE MUMMIES?

Ancient Egyptians believed in life after death. They wanted to preserve their bodies for the next life. A mummy is a dead body that has been dried and wrapped in strips of linen cloth, so that it will not rot.

WHY WERE THE PYRAMIDS BUILT IN EGYPT?

Thousands of years ago, Egyptians built pyramids as a place to bury their kings, called pharaohs [*fair*-oze]. When a pharaoh died, they put him inside the pyramid with his treasures.

WHY IS THE SPHINX SITTING IN THE DESERT IN EGYPT?

The Sphinx is a giant statue. It sits in front of the biggest pyramids in Egypt. The Sphinx has the head of a man and the body of a lion. Some experts think it's a statue of an Egyptian god. It could be guarding the pyramids. No one really knows.

WHY DID KNIGHTS JOUST?

A joust [*joust*] is a practice fight. In a joust, two knights on horses try to knock each other to the ground using lances. A lance is a long spear. Knights would joust for fun and practice. They were not trying to hurt each other.

X WHY Z

FACT:

In the days of kings and castles, jesters would put on funny shows. Jesters juggled, told stories, sang songs, and acted silly.

WHY DID KNIGHTS WEAR ARMOR?

When there were knights, there were no guns. Men fought with swords and spears. Steel armor could protect knights from these weapons. When soldiers began to use guns, armor could not protect them. That's why armor isn't worn anymore.

WHY DID KINGS AND QUEENS LIVE IN CASTLES?

Huge stone castles acted as forts to keep enemies away. Castles had guards and high walls. A big, important castle let people know how big and important the owner was.

WHY DOES THE AMERICAN FLAG HAVE 50 STARS?

The United States has 50 states. The flag has one star for each of the 50 states. When a new state joins our country, a new star is added to the flag.

50 STARS FOR 50 STATES

WHY DOES THE AMERICAN FLAG HAVE 13 STRIPES?

The 13 stripes stand for the 13 original colonies. The colonies were ruled by the British. Colonists declared their freedom in 1776.

13 STRIPES FOR 13 COLONIES

 FACT:

This is the first U.S. flag. It was made in 1777. Count the 13 stars and 13 stripes.

WHY DOES THE PRESIDENT LIVE IN THE WHITE HOUSE?

The White House was built more than 200 years ago to serve as the U.S. President's home and office. The President works downstairs in the Oval Office. The President's family lives upstairs. The White House is in Washington, D.C.

WHY DO WE VOTE FOR PRESIDENT EVERY FOUR YEARS?

When the United States began, Americans did not want a king. They wanted a leader chosen by the people. They thought four years was a good amount of time to be president.

WHY IS THE PRESIDENT CALLED THE COMMANDER-IN-CHIEF?

The President has many jobs. One job is to run the country. Another job is to be in charge of the Army, Navy, Marines, Air Force, and other military people. Because the President is chief of every soldier, his title is Commander-in-Chief.

WHY ARE THERE SO MANY CARS?

Not long ago, most Americans did not own a car. They lived in a town or city where it was easy to walk. But as cities became more crowded, many people wanted to move away. They wanted to live further from a city. They needed cars to get around.

WHY WAS THOMAS EDISON ABLE TO INVENT SO MANY THINGS?

Thomas Edison worked long hours in his lab. Plus, he had a lot of help. He started a factory where workers helped turn his ideas into inventions. Among his many inventions are the light bulb, the movie camera, and the phonograph (a machine that can record and play back sound).

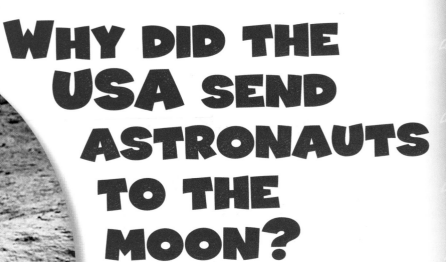

WHY DID THE USA SEND ASTRONAUTS TO THE MOON?

Beginning in 1957, there was a "space race" between the United States and the Soviet Union. Both countries wanted to be first to send men to the moon. It took many test rockets, but on July 20, 1969, two American astronauts landed on the moon and won the race.

X WHY Z FACT:

The first person to walk on the moon was Neil Armstrong.

INDEX

Photo Credits